MW01681000

HEBREWS

Study Guide

KEN YATES

Hebrews: Partners with Christ, Study Guide
Copyright © 2026 Grace Evangelical Society
P.O. Box 1308, Denton, TX 76202
Printed in the USA

Information requests should be directed to
ges@faithalone.org, www.faithalone.org

Yates, Kenneth 1958–

Design and typesetting by Lisa Simpson.

ISBN: 978-1-943399-82-6

All rights reserved. No part of this book may be reproduced
in any form without the prior permission of the publisher,
except as provided under US copyright law.

Scripture taken from the New King James Version.
Copyright © 1982 Thomas Nelson, Inc. Used by permission.
All rights resevered.

FOREWORD

In this study the words in bold type are taken directly from the book of Hebrews.

To prepare for each week's discussion, read the material to be covered enough times to become very familiar with it. In addition, answer the questions in the study, and write down any questions or points for discussion you would like to bring up with the study leader.

You may also want to consult commentaries such as: Hebrews: Partners with Christ by Ken Yates and/or Paul Tanner's chapter on Hebrews in *The Grace New Testament Commentary: Revised Edition*

TABLE OF CONTENTS

WEEK 1

Purpose and Overview of Hebrews

AUTHOR

While Hebrews does not identify its author, several suggestions have been made regarding the author's identity. These include Apollos, Luke, and the husband-and-wife team of Aquila and Priscilla. The very early church, however, mentions only two options: Paul or Barnabas.

There is early testimony from the church in the East that Paul wrote the book. In the West, there is an early witness to Barnabas's authorship. Interestingly, Barnabas is referred to as *a prophet* in Acts 13:1. While we cannot be dogmatic, it is best to follow the ancient witnesses and suggest that either Paul or Barnabas wrote the book.

The author of this study guide believes that Barnabas is the better alternative. In Heb 2:3-4, the author says that others had confirmed to him about the great salvation spoken of in Hebrews. These other people performed miracles to validate that teaching. Since Paul himself did miracles and received his teaching directly from the Lord, it seems unlikely that Paul would write these verses (Gal 1:11-16).

DATE

Hebrews must have been written before AD 95, as Clement of Rome refers to it in his writings of that period. In light of the book's indicating that sacrifices were being made in the temple at Jerusalem, the book must have been written before AD 70, the year when the temple was destroyed, and the sacrifices ceased (Heb 8:4; 10:1-2; 13:10).

The book could not have been written very soon after the beginning of the church (Acts 2), as the readers have been believers in Christ for some time (Heb 5:12-13). They do not appear to be part of the earliest generation of believers (2:3), which suggests a date between AD 50 and 70. Paul is not mentioned in the book. If he had died, Hebrews would have been written around AD 67-69.

ORIGINAL READERS

The first readers were from a Jewish background, but had become Christians. The author refers to them as "holy brethren" (3:1). The title of the book, "To the Hebrews," supports this, even though it was not part of the original letter. This title dates back to an early time and indicates that the early church believed the original readers were Jewish.

The book supports this view. The readers appear familiar with the Old Testament, its stories, and its sacrificial system. Their "fathers" were the Jews of the Old Testament (1:1).

The book offers additional suggestions regarding the readers' Jewish background. There is a heavy emphasis on angels in the book, and the readers believed these beings would rule the coming kingdom of God—a belief held by many Jews (1:4, 5; 2:5). The book of Hebrews is also the only New Testament book that discusses Melchizedek, a man we find in the book of Genesis and in Psalm 110 (5:10; chapter 7).

The author devotes considerable attention to the Old Testament Jews during their time in the wilderness. When he discusses the sacrificial system, he emphasizes the tabernacle in the wilderness rather than the temple in Jerusalem. He also discusses ritual washings, which were common in Judaism (6:2). The book emphasizes that Jesus is both King and High Priest, Jewish offices in the Old Testament.

During the first century, there were many different strands of Judaism. The Pharisees practiced the religion in one way, while the Sadducees practiced it differently. The Jews at Qumran, who wrote the Dead Sea Scrolls, had a different approach. The readers were probably heavily influenced by a group of Jews, similar to those found at Qumran, who emphasized Israel's time in the wilderness. Perhaps there were similar groups in different parts of the Roman Empire, and the original readers lived near one of them.

The readers had experienced persecution for their Christian faith (10:32-34). As a result, some had withdrawn from the church (10:25). They were tempted to return to Judaism, particularly the form of Judaism practiced by a specific sect within the religion.

This is what "sin willfully" refers to (10:26). It is something very specific. The author warns his readers not to publicly renounce their faith in Christ and return to the religion of their parents in order to avoid persecution. If they did, they would "fall away" (6:6), which refers to apostasy.

To renounce Christ would result in severe consequences. They needed to seriously consider what they were contemplating. Hebrews is famous for its "warning passages" that discuss these consequences.

Jesus was also their High Priest. They were familiar with that concept from Judaism. He would help them in their temptation to sin against Him as well as with their other difficulties. If they turned to Him, they would be greatly rewarded for their faithfulness to the King when He set up His Kingdom.

Hebrews compares Judaism and Christianity. Christianity is superior. Judaism was a shadow that pointed to the superior things that Christ brought. A shadow is inferior to the thing to which it points.

PURPOSE

The Epistle to the Hebrews tells readers that Jesus is the King of the world to come. He will rule over everything. Believers who are faithful to Him will rule with Him in His kingdom. That is, they will be His partners/companions (Grk. *metachoi*; cf. Heb 1:9; 3:14). If they renounce their faith, they will be in the kingdom but will lose eternal rewards (10:35; 11:35). They will also face God's discipline in this life.

The recipients of the Epistle to the Hebrews were experiencing difficulties, but they could turn to Christ, their High Priest. In Him, they would find the strength, grace, and mercy to remain faithful and to reign with Him (Heb 2:17-18; 4:14-16).

The warning passages in Hebrews deal with rewards. They do not threaten the loss of eternal life, which is impossible.

WEEK 1

QUESTIONS FOR DISCUSSION

1. **We do not know who authored the book of Hebrews. How does that affect the doctrine of inspiration of the Scriptures?**

2. **What kind of information provides the background for Hebrews? Why is the background information important?**

3. Why is it important to know whether the readers were believers, unbelievers, or a mixed audience?

4. In light of the book's purpose, why do you think the author presents Jesus as our King and High Priest?

5. What do you think Hebrews teaches believers about being unfaithful to the Lord?

6. What is apostasy, and what does Hebrews teach us about it?

7. There are five warning passages in Hebrews (2:1-4; 3:1–4:13; 6:4-8; 10:26-31; 12:25-29). Read over them. What do you think when reading them?

8. In what ways is Hebrews unique among all the books of the New Testament?

9. What do you have in common with the original readers?

10. What is the purpose of Hebrews? Defend your answer from the book itself.

WEEK 2:

The Prologue: Christ Is King (Hebrews 1:1-14)

The first four verses form the prologue. The author introduces the two offices of Jesus Christ: King and High Priest. If His people listen to Him, they will be greatly rewarded. If they disobey, there will be severe consequences. These themes will be seen throughout the book.

The rest of chapter 1 shows the greatness of this King.

Commentary

I. The Prologue (Heb 1:1-4)

1:1. God spoke to the Jews in the Old Testament through the **prophets** in **various** ways. This revelation was not complete. We can think of many ways God did this. He spoke in visions and dreams. He spoke to one prophet through a "still small voice" (1 Kgs 19:11-12). He even spoke to a false prophet through a donkey. Occasionally, He sent angels to teach His people.

1:2. Through Christ, God has **spoken** in **His Son**. Christ will inherit **all things**. This comes from Psalm 2, which speaks of the Messiah as King. He will rule over everything in His coming kingdom, since He created both the seen and unseen **worlds**.

1:3-4. Christ's greatness is seen in the **glory** of God that He showed in His miracles and on the Mount of Transfiguration. He is the exact **image**

of God (John 14:9). He is the final and perfect revelation of God. Nothing more will be said. Nothing more needs to be said. When someone looks at Christ, they see the Father (John 14:9). Not only is He our King and High Priest, but He is also the greatest Prophet who ever lived.

When He speaks, His people should listen. The **word of His power** holds the universe together. Great rewards will follow obedience. Discipline will follow disobedience.

But He is also our High Priest, who made the sacrifice for **our sins**. His sacrificial work is done, so He **sat down** at the **right hand** of God. He made the perfect sacrifice.

Such a King and High Priest is greater than the **angels**. Some Jews believed angels would rule the world to come. But no angel can compare to Him. He has a **name** that none of them have. It is the name of *Son*.

II. Christ, the King, Is Greater than the Angels (1:5-14)

To demonstrate that Jesus is the King and greater than the angels, the author appeals to the Old Testament. The Jewish Scriptures attest to these facts.

1:5. The name Jesus inherited is **Son**. No angel ever received that name. This verse comes from Ps 2:7, which speaks of the king of Israel. Those earthly kings foreshadowed the King to come. When Christ completed His work and ascended to the Father, He was declared the King of the world to come because He did all that was necessary for His people to enter that kingdom (Rom 1:4). Based on 2 Sam 7:14, the earthly kings of Israel, descendants of David, had God as their **Father**. Christ is the perfect King/Son.

1:6-7. When Christ returns, He will be the **firstborn**, which means that He will reign. In His kingdom, the **angels** will not rule but will **worship Him**. This comes from Ps 97:7. Psalm 104:4 says that angels are created **spirits**, and part of creation, like **fire**. They will serve the King.

1:8-9. Verses 8-9 quote from Psalm 45. Psalm 45:5-7 says that the King will defeat all His enemies and reign **forever and ever**. He will have a **righteous kingdom**. Psalm 45 is a wedding psalm. When the King reigns, it will be a time of joy. He will have **companions** (or partners). This refers to those who are close to the King. They will share in the joy of His reign. In Hebrews, this does not refer to all believers, but to believers who are close to the King. They will reign with Him. They will be like Him in that they loved righteousness. The word *partakers* (same word for "companion" here) is used in Heb 3:14. Being a companion of the Lord is being His partner in His reign.

1:10-12. Like Psalm 45, Psalm 102 says that the King will defeat all His enemies. Psalm 102:25-27 says that the King created the **earth** and the **heavens**. While Creation itself will **perish** and be **changed**, Christ will remain the **same**. He is eternal, and His kingdom will outlast this present universe when He creates a new heaven and earth.

1:13. None of the **angels** were ever told to **sit** at the **right hand** of God. This comes from Ps 110:1, which prophesies about the coming Christ. The Christ would also defeat all His **enemies**, a common theme of the Old Testament quotes in chapter 1.

1:14. Angels are **spirits** who serve not only the King, but also His companions (v 9). Christ will inherit all things, but angels minister to those who will **inherit salvation**. This means that angels have a special ministry to those believers who are faithful to the King. These believers will not only be in the eternal kingdom but will be greatly rewarded in it. This is the major thrust of the book of Hebrews.

This discussion of angels should have had a significant impact on the original readers, who were contemplating a return to Judaism and its elevated view of angels. They already had eternal life. If they remained faithful to Christ, they would rule in the coming kingdom. This was offered to human beings, not to angels.

Chapter 1 corrects a Jewish misunderstanding that angels will rule the world to come. Christ is the eternal King. When we believe in Jesus Christ for eternal life, we receive it as a free gift. However, Christ offers His people even more. He calls every believer to be one of His intimate companions in His kingdom. Christ will own the kingdom over which He rules, and He wants to give His followers a share in that inheritance. There is a difference between being in a place and inheriting that place. His faithful companions will inherit it. The book's readers should heed what the King says.

WEEK 2

QUESTIONS FOR DISCUSSION

1. **How does the prologue of Hebrews (Heb 1:1-4) support the doctrine of rewards?**

2. **Some have said that the prologue (vv 1-4) of Hebrews is one of the New Testament's most explicit statements that Jesus is God. Do you agree? Why or why not?**

3. In the Old Testament, the three great offices were prophet, priest, and king. How does chapter 1 show that Christ is the perfect fulfillment of all three?

4. The readers were tempted to leave Christianity and return to Judaism. How does the prologue show that Christianity is superior to Judaism?

5. In 1:5-14, the author quotes from many Old Testament passages. The context of these quotations is Christ's defeating all His enemies. The readers were being persecuted for their faith (10:32-34). Why does the author emphasize Christ's victory?

6. Who will Christ's "companions" (*metochoi*) be in the coming kingdom (v 9)? Compare other uses of *metochoi* in the New Testament (Luke 5:7; Heb 3:1, 14; 6:4; 12:8)?

7. In v 14, the author mentions "those who will inherit salvation [*sōtēria*]." Who are they? Compare other uses of *sōtēria* in Hebrews (2:3, 10; 5:9; 6:9; 9:28; 11:7).

8. What is the typical way in which people understand the role of angels considering v 14? How does a different view of "those who will inherit salvation" impact your understanding of what the author is saying about the role of angels in the lives of believers?

9. Look up the thirteen uses of the word *angels* in Hebrews. Why does the author talk so much about angels? (Angels are only mentioned more often in four NT books: Matthew, Luke, Acts, and the book that mentions them by far the most, Revelation.)

____

____

____

____

____

10. God the Father said to Jesus, "You are My Son. Today I have begotten You" (Heb 1:5, quoting Ps 2:7). Compare also Matt 3:17; 17:5; Mark 1:11; 9:7; Luke 3:22; 9:35; 2 Pet 1:17. What does this mean? Hasn't Jesus always been the Son of God?

____

____

____

____

____

WEEK 3

The First Warning Passage and Application (Hebrews 2:1-18)

Commentary

I. The Warning (2:1-4)

2:1-4. Chapter 1 ended with the word *salvation*. This refers to the deliverance that faithful believers will experience when Christ saves them from their enemies, and they rule with Him as His companions (1:9). It does not refer to salvation from hell.

The author warns his believing readers that they can **neglect** such a **great salvation** (v 3). He includes himself in that warning with the word **we**. Believers need to **heed** what the New Testament teaches about the great rewards for obedient believers in the coming kingdom. If we don't, we can **drift away** from sound teaching.

The Lord spoke of great rewards for faithfulness (Matt 5:3, 5, 7, 9-10; 25:34-35; Luke 6:20; 12:31-32; 22:29-30), and the Apostles **confirmed it**. They all did great **signs and wonders** (v 4), which testified to the truth of what they taught. **Disobedience** in the Old Testament brought a **just** punishment and loss of blessings (v 2). We can think of David, for example, who God severely disciplined when he committed adultery and murder. Believers will not **escape** such consequences if they do not obey (v 4). They will lose eternal rewards. God will also discipline them in this life.

II. Mankind Will Rule with Christ (2:5-18)

2:5-9. Christ did everything necessary to provide this salvation and allow faithful men and women to rule with Him in eternity. The eternal King became a Man so that mankind can reign.

Angels will not rule in the world to come, though many Jews thought they would (v 5). Instead, Psalm 8 says mankind will reign over creation (vv 6-8). While this psalm can describe man's current role in creation, it ultimately points to Christ's future role when He returns. All of creation will be subject to Him.

Christ became a Man and was made a little **lower than the angels** in the Incarnation. Christ, who is God (1:1-4), became a man so that He could experience **death** (v 9). Christ's death was an expression of the **grace of God**. Christ died for every single person. Since mankind experiences death, He identified with mankind through His death. If men and women are going to rule in an eternal kingdom, the King had to conquer death for them.

As a result of His death, He was **crowned with glory and honor** (v 9). Christ was obedient to His Father in the midst of suffering. As a result, God highly exalted Him. If the readers are obedient, God will exalt them as well.

2:10-16. Christ will rule over everything in the world to come. But He will also bring **many sons to glory**. This does not refer to all believers. These sons are the partners of Christ (1:9); they will inherit this salvation and reign with Christ (1:14). This inheritance is available to all Christians. While a believer can never lose eternal life and go to hell, he can neglect and lose his inheritance in God's kingdom (2:3).

The glory here does not refer to simply being saved from hell. *Glory* describes the authority in Christ's kingdom. He will share that glory with others. Faithful believers will share that glory and authority with Him. Believers will not all have the same glory in eternity.

He obtained His position after being faithful in His **sufferings**. Those who rule with Him will follow that example of obedience. He and His sons **are all of one**, because they share a common humanity. As an obedient Man, Christ showed us how to **trust** in God in the face of suffering.

In His death and resurrection, He set His people free from the **fear of death** (v 15). Satan can use the fear of death to tempt believers to fall away from the faith when they, like the original readers, are being persecuted. Faithful believers need not fear persecution, even if it leads to death. Christ suffered and experienced death as a Man. He had to become like human beings **in all things**. He had to be born, become tired, experience hunger and thirst, be tempted, and go through suffering and death. He can now give **aid** to believing men and women who come to Him. Since He knows what they are going through, He can be **merciful** to them.

2:17-18. He is our **faithful High Priest** (v 17) in the **things pertaining to God**. This means that He took care of **the sins of the people**. That is what a high priest does. He did all that was necessary to secure His people's relationship with God. He made His people holy (v 14). They can now approach God through their Great High Priest. He is faithful because He can be trusted to help any of His children who come to Him. If they are **tempted** to sin because of the difficulties they are going through, He will give them strength to endure.

The author introduces a fundamental idea. Our King is at the right hand of the Father (1:13). He is all-powerful. But He is also our High Priest. When His people approach Him, they find One who intercedes for them and who understands any suffering they experience.

And since He is all-powerful, **He is able to aid those who** come to Him. Christ Himself was **tempted** to sin. He was tempted to be unfaithful to God in the midst of difficulties. He knows what that is like. He can relate to the troubles of the original readers. They were tempted to give up. This is an appeal for them to go to Christ. They should not deny Him.

WEEK 3

QUESTIONS FOR DISCUSSION

1. **In the first warning passage, the readers are told about the danger of drifting away from what they had heard (v 1). What does that mean? What image does that create in your mind?**

2. **Many say that this warning passage (vv 1-4)—and all the warning passages in Hebrews—are addressed to false professors, i.e., those who lack "genuine" faith in Christ. How would you respond to that?**

3. **What punishment do you think the author of Hebrews has in mind for the believer who drifts away, and why doesn't the author spell it out?**

4. **What do you think about the author's discussion about angels and the role they will play in the world to come (v 5)?**

5. **In vv 6-8, the author quotes from Ps 8:4-6 regarding the role of man in God's creation. Is he talking about mankind in general, or the Man Jesus?**

6. **The author says that Christ had to be made perfect through suffering (v 10). How could the perfect Son of God be *made* perfect?**

7. **Verse 11 states that Jesus is "He who sanctifies [*hagiazō*]," and that the readers are "those who are being sanctified." What do you think the word *sanctified* means? Compare other uses of *hagiazō* in Hebrews (9:13; 10:10, 14, 29; 13:12).**

8. **In vv 11-12, the author repeats the word *brethren*, saying that Christ is not ashamed to call those who are sanctified by that name. What is the purpose of calling believers by this title?**

9. What does v 16 say about the possibility of fallen angels being saved from eternal condemnation in the lake of fire?

10. The author introduces the idea of Christ as our High Priest in vv 17-18. What does that mean for you as a believer?

WEEK 4

The Second Warning Passage (Hebrews 3:1–4:16)

In chapter 2, we were instructed to trust in God amid difficulties. Christ has given us the example to follow. We can go to Him for the help we need. But what if we don't? These chapters give an Old Testament example of God's people who did not remain faithful to God when confronted by their enemies. The original readers—and we—can benefit from their negative example.

Commentary

I. The Introduction (Heb 3:1-6)

3:1-6. The readers are called **holy brethren**. They have been sanctified by the blood of Christ (2:11). They are believers with a **heavenly calling** to reign with Christ in His kingdom as one of His close companions (1:9; 2:10). This calling is not a calling to be saved from hell.

Christ was **faithful** in what God told Him to do. So was **Moses**. God placed him over the tabernacle, a **house** of worship. But **Christ** is also over a **house** of worship as its High Priest over it (2:17-18). It is universal because the whole church worships in it. Believers around the world worship in Christ's house.

This house is not the Body of Christ, that is, the church itself. Just as there was priestly activity in Moses' house, so there is in the Christian church (13:10, 15-16). While a believer cannot remove himself from the Body of Christ and lose eternal life (Eph 1:13), a believer can withdraw from the house of Christ described here by ceasing to attend church with other believers and to worship God.

The option of withdrawing from this house is seen in the wording of the author's statement. Believers are members of the house over which Christ serves as High Priest, **if** they **hold fast**...**firm to the end**. The author again includes himself in this warning with the word ***we***. He knows that he could deny the faith if he doesn't hold fast to what he has been taught.

The author wants the readers to hold fast to the Christian confession (3:1). He wants them to hold fast to their **confidence**, which promises a great reward (10:35). This reward is to reign with Christ, which is also the **hope** spoken of in v 6. If we withdraw from worshipping God, we will lose this reward. That is what all the warning passages in Hebrews are about.

II. A Warning from the Old Testament (3:7-15)

3:7-11. The author quotes from Psalm 95, a psalm of worship. David refers to the Israelite **rebellion** in the **wilderness**. This concerns the period when the nation was instructed by God to enter the Promised Land and defeat its enemies. God had promised to give them the land (Numbers 22).

The people disobeyed, and God disciplined them for **forty years**. That **generation** died in the wilderness. They did not **enter** into God's **rest**. This rest does not refer to eternal salvation. For the Israelites, this *rest* meant more than simply entering the land. It involved possessing and owning it (Deut 3:18-20; 4:21; 12:8-10). In order to own the land, they had to defeat the enemies there. Their rest would involve rest from these enemies (Joshua 3–4). The Jews would not enjoy rest in the land until, *after* entering the land, they defeated all their enemies (Deut 25:19; Joshua 1:13; 21:43-45). To enter into God's rest required them to finish the work God had given them. If they did, then God would richly bless them.

The author applies David's warning in Psalm 95 to the people of his day, the original readers of Hebrews.

They have their enemies. But Christ has promised to defeat them (1:13). They also have an inheritance in the world to come. They can reign and possess that world with Christ (1:14; 2:3). It is their destiny to inherit all things (2:6-8).

But they have to finish their work. Some of the Jews at Kadesh were believers, and some were unbelievers. But they are used here as an illustration of God's people. They were part of the house of worship that Moses built (3:2). But they simply did not believe that God would keep His promise to deliver them when they faced great difficulties. This was true of both the believers and the unbelievers among the people. The nation as a whole withdrew from the battle. They paid a heavy price and experienced the discipline of God.

3:12-15. The author warns readers to **beware** (v 12)**;** they could do what the Jews in the wilderness did. As in 3:1, the readers are called **brethren**. They are Christians. But, like the Israelites, they could be guilty of **departing from the living God**.

A believer can believe some things but not others. A Christian can believe that he has eternal life in Christ, but not believe it is worth it to suffer for Him—that the rewards in the coming kingdom are worth the price he might have to pay in this life.

The readers would be doing that if they left Christianity and returned to Judaism. That would involve their not holding on to their Christian confession (3:1). It would include withdrawing from the "house" of worship over which Christ presides as our High Priest (3:1-6). They would not lose eternal life, but they would lose great rewards. God would discipline them.

The word **today** applies this warning to Christians in every age, including us. The day in which they live is the day they are put to the test.

III. An Explanation of Psalm 95 (3:16–4:13)

3:16-19. The Jews who **rebelled** were those whom God had brought out of **Egypt**. God was **angry** with them for **forty years**. They had **sinned** against God because they had not believed Him. They were still His people, but they did not believe He would give them victory over their enemies and bless them by giving them **rest** from their work and rewards in the land. Instead, God disciplined them by letting them die in the wilderness.

4:1-7. For the readers of Hebrews and Christians today, there is still the **promise of entering** God's **rest** (4:1). This is what is at stake and what can be lost. This verse includes a warning of the possibility of such loss. It is directed towards believers. The author says, "**let us fear.**"

The word *gospel* means "good news." Here, it does not refer to the message of eternal life. The Jews at Kadesh had good news—the **gospel—preached** to them. The good news was that God would bless them if they completed the works He had given them: to enter the land and to conquer it. Believers today have received good news. If we remain faithful to the Lord, we will **rest** from our works and be rewarded in His kingdom.

The word *believed* in the phrase "**we who have believed**" (4:3) is in the past tense. Those who have believed will enter that rest. In the context of the warning in Hebrews 3–4, we understand that this belief is not a one-time thing, such as when a person believes in Jesus Christ for eternal life. Instead, it is a belief that endures (3:6, 14). It is a belief that trusts in God during difficult times and when confronted by God's enemies. All Christians will be in the kingdom, but only those Christians who have believed in God's promises by remaining faithful to Him during difficult times will enter the reward of experiencing this rest and reigning with Christ.

4:8-11. The reward of entering this rest is offered to every generation of believers (4:9). It was not only for the Jews who, in the days of **Joshua**, did conquer the land; believers of any era who are faithful to God will be great in the kingdom.

Believers today could follow the tragic **example** of the Jews at Kadesh. The **word of God** helps us to avoid their error. God's word is **living** in the sense that it applies to all generations. Although the incident at Kadesh occurred thousands of years ago, and though David wrote his warnings in the Psalms thousands of years ago, these warnings apply to Christians today.

4:12-13. The Word of God is **powerful** because it produces results. It encourages, challenges, and warns people today. But it is also powerful because it pronounces judgment on God's wayward people.

God's word pronounced judgment on the Jews at Kadesh. He swore that they would not enter into the rest that was to have been their inheritance. The Word of God says that the disobedient believer, as well, will not enter His rest. At the Judgment Seat of Christ, every believer must give the Lord an **account** of how he lived. Believers who have been faithful will rule with Him.

IV. Conclusion (4:14-16)

4:14-16. Believers do not have to experience the judgment of God. We have a **High Priest**, Jesus Christ, who will give us all the help we need to remain faithful to Him. In the power He provides, we can **hold fast** to our Christian faith. He understands our **weaknesses** because He lived as a man (2:17-18).

The only logical thing to do is to go **boldly** to Him (v 16). Christians have the privilege of worshipping Christ in His house and of coming to Him whenever we want or whenever we have a need. We can approach

Him boldly because we know He understands what we are experiencing and can meet our needs.

And that is precisely what we find. Even though He is God, when we come to Him, we find Him on a **throne of grace**. The word *throne* reminds us that He is the King of the world to come. At that throne, the believer will find **mercy and help** in his **time of need**. Like the original readers, we should go to that throne.

WEEK 4

QUESTIONS FOR DISCUSSION

1. **Why is it significant that the readers are called "holy brethren" in v 1?**

2. **What is the "heavenly calling" these readers, and all believers, have (Heb 3:1)?**

3. What does it mean to be a part of Christ's house, as stated in Heb 3:6?

4. What are the "confidence...and hope" referred to in Heb 3:6?

5. In Heb 3:7-11, the author quotes from Ps 95:7-11, where David refers to what happened at Kadesh-Barnea. What happened there, and how does it relate to the purpose of the book of Hebrews?

6. **Do you think the Jews at Kadesh-Barnea represent believers or unbelievers? Why?**

7. **In 3:12, the author warns the readers about having an "evil heart of unbelief." What does this refer to?**

8. **What is the *rest* (4:1) that is available for the original readers and for all believers?**

9. According to Heb 4:12-13, what role do the Scriptures play in helping the believer become a partner with Christ in the world to come?

10. Why do you think the author concludes this long warning passage with a discussion about the high priesthood of Christ (4:14-16)?

WEEK 5

Jesus Is Our High Priest (Hebrews 5:1-14)

Commentary

Hebrews 1–4 focuses on Jesus as the Son, indicating that He is the King of the world to come. Now, the author focuses on Jesus as our High Priest. He introduced this theme at the end of chapter 4. All believers will be in the kingdom. But if the believer wants to rule with the King, he must go to Him as his High Priest.

I. The Requirements for Being a High Priest (Heb 5:1-4)

5:1-4. The book is written to people who knew the Old Testament. The author speaks of the Old Testament's requirements for a **high priest**. He had to be a human being and represent men in **things pertaining to God**. He was man's representative before God. This involved offering **sacrifices for sins** to God on behalf of those he represented.

The Old Testament high priest was also required to have **compassion for** the people. Even though he was not to condone sin, he represented sinners who would sometimes go **astray**. He knew that he was also a sinner, **subject to weakness** in this area. Therefore, he would need to offer sacrifices for the sins of both the **people** and **himself**.

Another Old Testament requirement was that the high priest had to be **appointed** by God. He could not simply take the **honor** because he wanted it. In the Old Testament, **Aaron** was chosen by God as the first high priest. God said that from then on, only Aaron's descendants could serve in that capacity.

Since the author has just said that Christ is our High Priest (4:15-16), the natural question is: Did Christ meet all these requirements?

II. Christ Met All the Requirements for Being Our High Priest (Heb 5:5-10)

5:5-6. The author discusses the requirements in vv 1-4 and shows that Jesus met all of them. He did not **glorify Himself** by appointing Himself to the office of **High Priest**. His Father appointed Him.

This is seen in Ps 110:4. In that psalm, God says of the Messiah, the Son, "**You are a priest forever.**" The Father appointed the Son as both the King and the High Priest of His people.

Since Christ is both King and High Priest, He is the fulfillment of another Old Testament figure, **Melchizedek**. The author will later discuss how Melchizedek was both a king and a priest.

Among the Jews, a man could not be both a high priest and a king. High priests came from the tribe of Levi. Kings came from the tribe of Judah. If Christ was both, He was greater than any Jewish high priest.

We also see that He is greater because He was appointed a High Priest **forever**. No Jewish high priest could make that claim. All of them died and therefore had to be replaced. Christ exceeded the requirements for an Old Testament high priest. None of them served forever.

5:7-10. As a High Priest, Christ **offered** up sacrifices to God (v 7). The same word for *offered* is used in v 7 and v 1.

Jesus offered **up prayers and supplications**. Prayers are a form of sacrifice (13:15). The term for *supplication* denotes someone who humbly asks God for something. But when did Christ do that, and what did He ask for?

This occurred when Christ offered up prayers **to Him who was able to save Him from death**. Christ offered this prayer with **cries and tears**. This would include when He was in the Garden of Gethsemane and when He was on the cross. His prayers were **heard**, even though He died on the cross. His Father showed that He heard Him by raising Him from the dead. His Father "saved Him from death." He also offered Himself on the cross as a sacrifice for His people (1:3; 2:11).

Jesus was heard because He was holy. His sacrifice of Himself was acceptable to God for the same reason. Because of His righteousness, He can sit at the right hand of the Father (1:13).

While on earth, the Father heard the Son. Now, the Son is also our High Priest. He is our representative before the Father, in His very presence. When He intercedes with the Father for us (4:14-16), does the Father hear Him on our behalf? The answer is obvious. The believer who goes to Christ knows that God will hear Christ's intercession on behalf of that believer.

As the High Priest of men, He is a man. He took on **flesh**. He was able to offer up Himself in death as a sacrifice because He became a man.

As a man, He can have compassion on those He represents. He **suffered** as a man. He **learned**, experientially, what **obedience** to the Father involves. He knows what it means to be faithful to God in times of trouble and persecution. He knows what His people go through. Through this process, He has been **perfected** for His role as our High Priest.

As such a high priest, He is **the author of eternal salvation to all who obey Him** (v 9). This is not salvation from hell. That salvation is a gift. Here, the author of Hebrews addresses the salvation granted to those who remain faithful to Christ in this world and will therefore reign with Him when He returns (2:3). One must obey Him to obtain it. Believers already have eternal life. Now they can go to Him to obtain another kind of salvation.

He is the *author* of this salvation because He paved the way. He was obedient, and the Father exalted Him to the position of extreme and eternal authority at His right hand (1:13). His people must draw near to Him (4:14-16) to find the help they need.

III. Introduction to the Warning (5:11-14)

5:11-14. A believer cannot approach the Lord as his High Priest if he denies Him. The believer who denies the Lord will still have eternal life, but he will not go to Him for the strength he needs in order to obtain the eternal salvation of reigning with Christ. The next warning appears in the next chapter, where the author introduces the danger the readers face.

The readers needed to know how Christ is both King and High Priest, but such things are **hard to explain**. The readers had become **dull** in their ability to understand spiritual things, such as rewards in the world to come. The word *dull* means "to be sick." We are reminded of the first warning passage (2:1-4). If believers are not careful, they can drift away from spiritual truth and health.

They had been believers long enough to have become **teachers** of such things, but instead, they needed to be taught the basics. They were infants in their understanding, able to take in only the **milk** of God's Word. They were **unskilled**, which means they did not put into practice what the Word said about suffering with Christ and the reality of rewards.

If they put such doctrinal truths to the test in their lives, they would mature. They could go to their High Priest for the help they needed, and He would provide it. They would then be able to **discern between good and evil**.

This refers to both good and evil doctrine. Some of the believers were not able to recognize the stark differences between Judaism and Christianity. In addition, they were faced with persecution because of their faith. In times like that, spiritual immaturity is especially dangerous.

These verses show the importance of doctrine. Believers can differ on minor issues. But there are fundamental doctrines that we must hold on to. Some of the readers reasoned that as long as they worshipped God—whether in a meeting with Christians or in a synagogue—what difference did it make? They needed to understand that doctrines that address the fundamentals of our faith cannot be discarded without serious consequences.

This explains why the author of Hebrews repeatedly urges them to hold fast to their Christian faith (3:6, 14; 4:11). They were in danger of making wrong decisions because the ability to make right decisions often depends on spiritual maturity. The spiritually immature believer is in danger of doing things that will cause him to experience God's discipline and the loss of eternal rewards.

Some of the readers were in that situation. Some immature believers had already publicly renounced their faith. Some believers who remained were now considering doing the same thing.

WEEK 5

QUESTIONS FOR DISCUSSION

1. **What were the requirements for being a high priest in the Old Testament (Heb 5:1-4)?**

2. **The author says that the Old Testament high priest is a type of Christ because he pointed to the Lord. What other Old Testament types pointed to Christ?**

3. In Heb 5:5-6, the author introduces two reasons for Christ's being greater than any Old Testament high priest. What are they?

4. While on earth, Christ was *heard* by His Father. What does this mean for believers today?

5. In Heb 5:7, the author refers to "the days of His [Christ's] flesh." How does that relate to His being our High Priest, and what does it mean for us?

6. How could Christ, who is God, learn obedience? Why did He need to be *perfected* (Heb 5:8-9)?

7. How many times does the expression *eternal salvation* occur in the rest of the Bible? List all the verses. Does the fact that this is a rare expression suggest that maybe we should refer to *everlasting life*, rather than *eternal salvation,* when evangelizing? Why or why not?

8. How do we know that the *eternal salvation* in v 9 is not talking about salvation from the lake of fire?

9. **What do vv 11-14 tell us about the danger of Christian immaturity?**

10. **In 5:13-14, how does the author of Hebrews describe the process of Christian growth? Can you think of experiences in your life that brought about such growth?**

WEEK 6

The Third Warning Passage (Hebrews 6:1-20)

Chapter 5 concluded with the statement that the readers have not progressed to maturity in their Christian lives. The author now warns about what can happen. It is one of the strongest warnings in the New Testament.

Commentary

I. Press on to Maturity (6:1-3)

6:1-3. The author encourages the readers, and himself, to move past the milk of the Word (5:12) and to press on to maturity or **perfection**. This would enable them to take in solid food from the Word (5:11-14).

He lists some of the basics of the faith and how they differ from Judaism. The first is **repentance from dead works**. When they practiced Judaism, they sought to gain acceptance before God through works of the Law and the sacrifices required in the Old Testament. But all these are dead in the sense that they cannot bring life. Christianity taught them that Christ put an end to all the rituals and that the Law cannot give life. Only the Spirit can.

Unfortunately, some take this statement about repentance and teach that repentance is necessary for salvation from the lake of fire. They say that one must repent, or turn from his sins, before he can be saved. However, the author is not discussing turning away from the dead works of sin. He is referring to religious works that lack spiritual value.

This life is given by the second fundamental discussed here: **faith toward God**. To believe in God is to believe in the One He sent, Jesus Christ (John 12:44). If they deny the Christian faith, they will not have faith toward God.

Forsaking the fundamentals of Christianity would necessitate a return to dead works. They would then need to turn, or repent, from the fundamentals of Judaism.

Judaism also differed from Christianity in other doctrines. The readers should move beyond these basics toward maturity. God **permits** such growth to occur.

II. The Consequences of Falling Away (6:4-8)

6:4-8. There is no doubt that vv 4-5 describe believers. If a Christian does not mature, he can **fall away** from the faith. Some of the readers had done that.

But what can be said about such believers? It is impossible **to renew them again to repentance**. Once again, we see that the author is talking to Christians. They have already repented. If they fall away, they will need to repent again.

The *repentance* here has nothing to do with believing in Jesus for eternal life. *Repentance* is not the same thing as *faith*. *Repentance* means "to turn away from" something. It is undoubtedly best to take it here in the same sense as in v 1. When the readers were Jewish unbelievers, they thought acceptance before God was based upon keeping the Jewish Law and rituals. When they believed in Jesus Christ for eternal life, they saw that acceptance before God was based upon faith. They had repented from the dead works of another system, that is, works that can never give life. They repented from trusting in the works of the Law and instead believed in Christ for eternal life. If they returned to Judaism and that system of worship, then they would need to turn from it again.

But what can be said to such a person? What can another Christian say to him? The person who falls away from the faith already knows the truth. It would be impossible for us to get this person to see the error of his ways and turn away from a system that cannot give life or that is not pleasing to God as a system of worship. If their turning away happens, God will do it through the discipline He brings into that believer's life. The apostate believer deserves such discipline because he has publicly put

Christ to **shame**. It is shameful to the cause of Christ when one of His children denies Him before the eyes of the world.

God's discipline is described by making a comparison between a field that produces good fruit and a field that does not. A field that produces good fruit—obviously meant to represent a faithful believer—receives **blessing from God**. An apostate believer is like a field that produces **thorns and thistles**. The farmer burns such a field to eliminate harmful growth.

Such an action constitutes cursing. In the Bible, this does not refer to eternal damnation, but to God's discipline. This can happen to His people (Deut 28–30). The burning here can picture the loss of rewards the apostate believer will experience (1 Cor 3:10-15). The burning is not a picture of the lake of fire. Even in the illustration, the field is not destroyed.

III. A Call to Hold on (6:9-12)

6:9-12. The author is **confident** that his readers will not experience such discipline from God. They have been faithful in the past, and he expects them not to be **sluggish**, meaning "sick," in their spiritual growth. Instead, he wants them to remain faithful to the Lord and to **inherit the promises** that mature believers who went before them will inherit. These promises include reigning with Christ and being great in His kingdom.

IV. Conclusion to the Warning (6:13-20)

6:13-20. Abraham is an example of a believer who received the **promise** of God's blessings because of his faithfulness. It was the promise of rewards, not of eternal salvation. When he received this promise of rewards, Abraham already had eternal life.

He received the promise of rewards in Genesis 22. Abraham was saved spiritually in Genesis 15. In other words, when God made this promise of rewards to Abraham, Abraham had already been saved from hell for many years. He received this new promise only *after* he had obeyed God.

In Genesis 22, the promise was made to Abraham immediately after he demonstrated his willingness to sacrifice his son, Isaac, as an offering to God. God tested Abraham to see whether he would obey in the midst of a severe trial.

God promised that Abraham would receive a **blessing**. This blessing included many things. God was going to **multiply** him so that he would have an innumerable number of descendants. From Gen 22:16-18, we also see that in Abraham, all the nations of the earth would be blessed. In addition, his descendants would inherit the cities of their enemies. The fact that this promise included an inheritance and a victory over the enemies of God's people would be very relevant to the readers of Hebrews (1:13–2:4).

These blessings were given to Abraham only **after he had patiently endured**. This is what the readers—and we—are encouraged to do (v 12).

WEEK 6

QUESTIONS FOR DISCUSSION

1. **Verse 2 says that the resurrection of the dead and eternal judgment are part of the basics of Christian teaching. What does the New Testament teach about these things, and how would it differ from what the Pharisees and Sadducees believed?**

2. **Many say that all "true" believers grow, or mature, in the faith. How would you respond to that view in light of Heb 5:12–6:8?**

3. Some say that Heb 6:4-6 is talking about unbelievers. How would you argue that the author is talking about believers?

4. How does the believer who denies the faith "crucify again for [himself] the Son of God" (Heb 6:6)?

5. In 6:5-6, the author talks about believers who apostatize. In 6:7-8, he uses an illustration comparing fruitful land with fruitless land "whose end is to be burned." How does "whose end is to be burned" apply to apostate believers?

6. How does Hebrews 6:8 allude to Gen 3:17-18. Be specific.

7. In Heb 6:9-10, what are some indications that the author is writing to believers, even though he has just given them a strong warning?

8. How does Heb 6:11-12 prove that not all believers will mature in their faith until the end of their lives?

9. In Heb 6:12, the readers are told that they can inherit promises. How do we know this does not refer to going to heaven?

10. How would you apply this warning passage to people today?

WEEK 7

Jesus and Melchizedek (Hebrews 7:1-28)

The author has just warned the readers about denying the faith (6:1-11). The key to holding on to their faith is that Jesus is our High Priest. Because the readers were contemplating a return to Judaism, the author compares Christ to the Old Testament Jewish high priests. He has said that Christ is a High Priest like Melchizedek (6:20). The author will show that Christ is greater than Old Testament high priests by showing the greatness of Melchizedek.

Commentary

I. The Greatness of Melchizedek (7:1-10)

7:1-4. Melchizedek has a small role in the Old Testament. In Genesis 14, some foreign kings defeated the people around the Dead Sea and took slaves, including Abraham's nephew Lot. Abraham pursued the kings and defeated them.

When Abraham returned, he was met by Melchizedek, the **king of Salem**. Melchizedek **blessed** Abraham, and Abraham paid a tithe to him. Melchizedek was a **priest of the Most High God**. He was both a king and a priest. Nobody else in the Old Testament was both.

His greatness is seen in the fact that he had no parents or **beginning of days**. He was probably an angel. Since he didn't die, he **remains a priest continually** (v 3). No Old Testament priest could say that.

7:5-10. Melchizedek was greater than Abraham and **Levi**, who was a descendant of Abraham and the father of all the priests in the Old Testament. Melchizedek was greater than any Old Testament priest.

II. The Need for a New High Priest (7:11-19)

7:11-13. The Jews were under the Old Covenant given through Moses. It had its own **priesthood**, from the tribe of Levi, which offered sacrifices for the sins of the people.

But this system did not bring **perfection**. It did not fully address the issue of sin among God's people. Something new and better was needed.

God spoke of a **need** for **another priest**. He would be like **Melchizedek rather** than **Aaron**, from whom the Old Testament priests descended.

If God was satisfied with the old system, why did He speak of the need for a new high priest? If this **priesthood** was **changed**, then there must also be a **change of the law** itself (v 12). The whole Old Covenant would have to be replaced.

7:14-19. Christ brought a change regarding the priesthood. He did not come from the **tribe** of Levi. Instead, He was from the tribe of **Judah**.

The Old Testament, in Ps 110:4, said that the Messiah would be like **Melchizedek**. He would be **another** kind of **priest**. He would be different from the priests who descended from Levi, including Aaron, the first high priest. He would be both a king and a priest.

The Old Testament priests were men of flesh, descended from other men. They died, so descendants were needed to take their place. But Christ is greater because His priesthood is based upon **an endless life**. He needed no descendants (4:14-16). Psalm 110 said that He would be a **priest forever** (v 17). He would be a priest **according to the order of Melchizedek**, not Levi. Christ is greater than Levi.

A change for the better has taken place. The old has been set aside or **annulled**. The new is better because the old was characterized by **its weakness and unprofitableness** (v 18). The old did not give the worshipper a clear conscience before God or the ability for the worshipper to boldly approach God with confidence (4:14-16). This ability enables the New Testament believer to **draw near to God** through Christ, finding the strength to endure and to reign with Him. This is the believer's **hope**.

III. The Greatness of Jesus Christ (7:20-28)

7:20-25. Three things make Christ greater than the Old Testament high priests: an oath, the eternality of His office, and His character.

In Psalm 110, God took an **oath** saying that the Messiah would be a High Priest. That did not happen with the Old Testament priests.

Psalm 110 also says that Christ is a priest **forever**. This was something else that the Old Testament priests could not claim. They died and remained buried. **Jesus** is the **surety**—He guarantees—all the blessings of the New **Covenant**.

In the Old Testament, a high priest might be good and care for the people, but eventually, he would die. The one who replaced him might be an immoral man. But Christ, the perfect High Priest, never dies. Christians always have Him as their Representative before the Father.

Christ is able to **save to the uttermost** every believer. This does not refer to salvation from hell. He can save them completely, which refers to what was said in 1:14 and 2:1-4: Believers who go to Him will be saved through trials and from their enemies. They will be one of Christ's partners and reign with Him forever. As the believers' High Priest, He intercedes for all who come to Him for help (4:14-16).

7:26-28. Christ is also qualified to be our High Priest because of His character. He is **holy**. He is **harmless**, which probably means that He did not commit any evil.

He is **undefiled**, which probably means that the sacrifice He made as our High Priest (on the cross) was a perfect sacrifice, completely acceptable to God. Christ is also **separate from sinners**, ascended to God in the **heavens** (1:13). This does not mean that He is inaccessible, since the author tells us to go to Him boldly. It means that in Him there is no sin.

No Old Testament priest could claim these things. That is why they had to make repeated sacrifices. They had to make sacrifices for their own sins. But Christ did not have to make a sacrifice for His sins, because He had none. For His people, He made one sacrifice of Himself **once for all**.

Our High Priest **has been perfected forever**. As we saw in chapter 2, He is our perfect High Priest because He became a man and knows what it means to suffer. He can therefore sympathize with us. But He is also perfect because of the perfect sacrifice of Himself.

It would be foolish for the readers to reject this High Priest and turn back to the Jewish system and its priests.

WEEK 7

QUESTIONS FOR DISCUSSION

1. **What do you think the author means when he says that Melchizedek had no parents, no beginning of days, and no end of life?**

2. **In what ways did Melchizedek point to Christ?**

3. According to Heb 7:11, why was the Old Covenant, based upon the Law of Moses, replaced by Christ?

4. How does the coming of Christ show that the Law of Moses has been replaced?

5. What does the author mean by a "better hope" in Heb 7:19? And what does *hope* mean in the New Testament?

6. **The section covered by Heb 7:20-28 begins and ends with a reference to God's oath concerning Christ. What is the significance of this oath?**

7. **In v 22, the author says that Jesus is the *surety* of a better covenant, which means that He is the guarantee. What does the Lord guarantee?**

8. **In v 25, what does the author mean when he says that Christ is able to save His people "to the uttermost," and how is His intercession for us related to this salvation?**

9. In v 26, the author describes the kind of High Priest Christ is for the believer and says that He is *fitting* for us. What do you think this means?

10. How was Jesus' death on the cross different than the daily and annual sacrifices that were made under the Law (v 27)? Why is the Roman Catholic view of communion and the crucifix a misrepresentation of Christ offering Himself up?

WEEK 8

Christ Has Brought the Better Things (Hebrews 8–9)

In chapter 7, we saw that Christ is better than the high priests of the Old Testament. In chapters 8–9, we see that He is superior in other ways. He brought in a better covenant, a better sacrifice, better promises, and a better sanctuary. Why would anybody go back to the inferior, old versions of these?

Commentary

I. Christ's Superior Ministry (8:1-6)

The Old Testament priests ministered in a **sanctuary** on earth. Christ ministers for His people in the **true tabernacle** in the heavens, seated at the right hand of God. The Old Testament priests offered **sacrifices** in the earthly tabernacle. But their tabernacle and sacrifices were only **shadows** of the **heavenly things**. They pointed to the real thing that was to come. As shadows, they have passed away.

Christ did all that was necessary to bring in a **better covenant** and **better promises**. The Old Testament speaks of eternal rewards, and the New Testament speaks of earthly blessings that result from obedience. But the promises in the Law of Moses pertained mainly to earthly blessings. The promises of Christ are directed mainly toward the kingdom and eternal blessings.

II. The Superiority of the New Covenant (8:7-13)

8:7-10. Even the Old Testament said that the Old Covenant was going to be replaced. The Old Testament prophet Jeremiah, who lived about 600 years before Christ, said the **days are coming** when God would make a **new covenant** with Israel. The Jews were not able to keep the Old Covenant. In Jeremiah's day, God had to discipline the nation and send the people into exile because they did not keep His commandments.

8:11-13. The New Covenant will be with the **house of Israel**. This is not with the church. In the Old Testament, not every Jew was a believer. When the Lord returns and sets up His kingdom, the nation will be under that covenant. Every Jew will **know the Lord**. They will all be believers. They will not need to make sacrifices for **their sins**. God will **remember their sins no more**. That was not the case under the Old Covenant. Both believers and unbelievers in the nation needed to make sacrifices in order to avoid the discipline of God.

Christ did all that was necessary to bring in the New Covenant for Israel. With His coming, the Old Covenant has become **obsolete**. He put an end to it. Why would the readers consider trying to worship God under it?

III. The Inferior Tabernacle (9:1-10)

9:1-5. The author has spoken about the earthly tabernacle in the Old Testament. This was the tabernacle used by the Jews in the wilderness. He now speaks of how it was inferior to the one in which Christ serves.

The Old Testament tabernacle was an **earthly** building, made of earthly materials. It had two rooms. The larger room contained a **lampstand**, a **table** with bread for the priests, and a **golden censer** that burned incense.

The inner room, the Holy of Holies, had the **ark of the covenant**, which was covered in **gold**. It contained certain items, including the **tablets of the covenant**, which contained the Law of Moses written on stone by the finger of God.

As impressive as these furnishings were, they were all temporary. That is the main point the author wants to make. In v 4, he mentions that many of these things were made of **gold**. Gold, though valuable, still belongs to this world. Whatever these objects picture, they are just that: a picture. Christ, on the other hand, serves in the real tabernacle and the presence of God. He serves in the heavenlies, not on earth.

9:6-10. The Old Testament priests would serve in the **first** room. The **high priest** could enter the Holy of Holies **once a year**. But he had to offer a sacrifice for **himself and for the people's sins**. The Holy of Holies represented the presence of God on earth. The people of God could not enter into God's presence as long as that **tabernacle** stood.

The **sacrifices** offered there did not take care of sins once and for all. They could not clear the **conscience**. The sacrifices involved only outward actions, such as ritual **washings**.

IV. The Perfect Has Arrived in Christ (9:11-22)

9:11-15. Christ, as our **High Priest**, serves us in the **perfect tabernacle** not of this world. He does not serve us with the **blood** of animals, but with His own blood—the blood of the God who became a Man. He does not enter into the Holy of Holies only once a year; He has entered it **once for all**. With one sacrifice, His blood redeemed His people forever.

The services at the Old Testament tabernacle involved the cleansing of physical objects. The blood of Christ cleanses us spiritually and internally, giving us a clear **conscience** since we know that the sacrifice for our sins was taken care of by His one sacrifice.

With this clear conscience, we can **serve the living God**. Christ, at the right hand of God, is the **Mediator** between God and us. He is our perfect High Priest.

Christ's death was so great that it took care of the sins, or **transgressions, under the** Old Covenant. In the Old Testament, the blood of animals only *covered* the sins of His people. Christ's sacrifice on the cross would provide the blood that would *take away* those sins.

9:16-22. Moses established the first covenant with the **death** and the **blood** of animals. This death put the covenant into effect. He placed the blood on the tabernacle and its furniture. It "cleansed" it so it could serve the needs of the people. The blood was also used to cleanse the priests for service. Blood was used for all aspects of the religious needs of God's people. This all points to the inferiority of the Old Covenant compared with what Christ has provided.

V. Christ's Superior Sacrifice (9:23-28)

9:23-26. Christ's superior tabernacle would require a greater sacrifice than that of animals. Christ's death makes possible the High Priestly ministry that He performs at the right hand of God. He serves in the real **presence of God for us**. The blood of animals could not do that. His sacrifice was so great that it only needed to be offered **once for all**. No more sacrifice for sin is needed. No other sacrifice could be made. Since the animal sacrifices did not atone for sin, they had to be offered repeatedly. They continually reminded the worshipper of something greater that was to come.

9:27-28. All men **die**. Since Christ was a Man, He also died **once**. But Christ is different from all other men in an important way. After men die, they face a **judgment**. Believers will be judged at the Judgment Seat of Christ to determine their rewards in the kingdom of God. Unbelievers face judgment at the Great White Throne, where they will be cast into hell.

Christ will not be judged, but will bring **salvation**. This does not refer to salvation from hell. All believers already have eternal life, but not all believers eagerly wait for Him and His kingdom. The *salvation* of v 28 will be given when Christ comes for His people the **second time**. This salvation is for those **who eagerly wait for** His coming.

Paul referred to this when he spoke of those believers who love the Lord's appearing (2 Tim 4:8). They will receive a crown, which is a special reward.

In the context of the book of Hebrews, Christians who eagerly look for Christ's return are those who hold fast to their Christian confession and hope (3:14; 4:1; 5:9; 6:13-20). They receive a salvation, or deliverance, from their enemies (1:14). Christ will exalt them. This salvation will include the reward of an inheritance in God's kingdom (9:15). They will reign with Christ.

The death of Christ and His service as our High Priest provide what we need to obtain this kind of salvation.

WEEK 8

DISCUSSION QUESTIONS

1. **Hebrews 8:5 says that the Old Testament tabernacle was "a copy and shadow." What does this mean, and why was this significant for the original readers?**

2. **What are the "better promises" of the "better covenant" in Heb 8:6?**

3. **Why did God find "fault" with the Law of Moses (8:8)?**

4. **What does Heb 9:1-5 teach us about making idols of things made of earthly materials?**

5. **What does it mean that the "way into the Holiest of All was not yet made manifest" while the tabernacle was standing?**

6. **The Law of Moses and the sacrifices it commanded are said to have involved "fleshly ordinances" (Heb 9:10). What does that mean?**

7. **What is the eternal inheritance in Heb 9:15?**

8. **In Heb 9:24-26, the author gives two ways in which Christ's sacrifice was greater than the Old Testament sacrifices. What are they?**

9. What kind of judgment will the believer experience after he dies (or is caught up in the Rapture) (Heb 9:27)?

10. Is Heb 9:27 about the judgment of believers only, or of all people? Defend your answer.

WEEK 9

The Fourth Warning Passage (Hebrews 10:1-39)

In Heb 8:1–9:28, the author explained how Christ is superior to the Old Testament priests and has a superior ministry. His death is the basis for a superior covenant. His sacrifice is superior to the Old Testament sacrifices. In 10:1-18, we see the results of His superior sacrifice. This leads to the book's fifth warning. It is addressed to those who would abandon Christ's ministry and return to the old system.

Commentary

I. The Inferiority of the Old Testament Sacrifices (vv 1-4)

10:1-4. The Law of Moses was only a **shadow** and pointed to the **good things** that would come later. The sacrifices under the Law were not able to **make** the worshipper **perfect**. They pointed to the real thing that God would later bring. The perfect sacrifice that God desired would take care of sin once for all.

Under the Law, sacrifices had to be offered every year because the **blood** of animals cannot **take away sins**. They pointed to the sacrifice that would.

II. Christ's Sacrifice Accomplished God's Will (vv 5-18)

10:5-10. Christ took on a human **body** in order to be the sacrifice that accomplished God's will for His people. The result of Christ's sacrifice is that His people are **sanctified once for all**. His death is the basis for the forgiveness of sin, including all our sins. Because Christ died for the sins of the world, He can give eternal life to all who believe in Him for it. At the moment of faith, we are declared holy. When a person believes, all his past sins are forgiven. When a believer sins and confesses those sins, they are forgiven through the death of Christ.

10:11-18. Christ's sacrifice accomplished the **will** of God for His people. The sacrifices of the **first** covenant could not do that. God's people have been **perfected** in the sense that they know the sacrifice that gives them complete access to God has been made. There is now no **longer** any **offering for sin**. Christ has done it all.

Anybody who goes to the sacrifices of Judaism will go to a system that cannot offer the forgiveness of sins.

III. The Warning (vv 19-31)

10:19-24. Believers should take full advantage of the access to God that Christ's death provides. We can go to Him with **boldness**. The Christian readers should **hold fast to** their **hope** of reigning with Christ. He has **promised** to give them rewards if they do so. One way they can hold fast is to continue meeting with other believers and encouraging **one another**.

10:25-28. If they chose to stop meeting with other believers, as **some** had already done, they would be sinning **willfully**. The willful sin, in this context, does not refer to the believer who sins when he knows he is being disobedient to the Lord. It refers to the believer who denies the faith. To reject Christ would be to reject the only sacrifice that can provide access to God, which gives them the strength necessary for remaining faithful. There is no other **sacrifice**, including the animal sacrifices provided by Judaism. The apostate believer can only expect the **judgment** of God. God will discipline Him.

10:29. This discipline can be **worse** than death. It does not involve going to hell, since that is impossible for the believer. The discipline may involve physical punishment that the believer experiences now. It will definitely involve the loss of eternal rewards. The punishment is deserved because of the way the apostate believer has treated the **Son of God**. These verses are not talking about what happens to unbelievers, but to the **people**

of God whom He will judge. This judgment will take place in this life as well as at the Judgment Seat of Christ, when eternal rewards will be given for faithfulness.

The Bible gives many examples of how God judged His own people. He often took the lives of believers. In the book of Hebrews, we are reminded of how God severely judged the nation of Israel at Kadesh-Barnea. Some of those who died in the wilderness were believers. Other examples include Nadab and Abihu (Lev 10:1-3), Ananias and Sapphira (Acts 5:1-11), and certain believers at Corinth (1 Cor 11:30). James ends his book with a warning that God can take the life of a believer who falls into sin (Jas 5:20).

The warning here involves a fiery punishment (v 27). Many see that word (fiery) and think it means "hell." But the author alludes to Isa 26:11 and Deut 32:35. In those Old Testament passages, *fire* does not refer to hell. It refers to the wrath that the Lord pours out on both His enemies and His people when they act like His enemies. God's anger is directed at His people who rebel against Him. It can be described as the *fire* of His wrath.

Once again, the author speaks of the believer as one who is **sanctified** (v 29; vv 10, 14). At the moment a person believes in Jesus Christ for eternal life, many spiritual changes occur. The person receives eternal life and can never lose it. The death of Christ makes that possible. But the death of Christ is also the basis for our justification. Positionally, the believer is set apart in God's eyes as His child. He is declared righteous by Him. He has access to our High Priest. In Him, we can receive the forgiveness of all our sins. This makes intimacy with the Father possible. What will happen if the believer—who has received all these blessings because of the death of Christ—denies Him?

10:30-31. In Deuteronomy 32, God describes what He will do to His people, Israel, if they fall into idolatry. His **vengeance** will include things like disease, plagues, and defeat at the hands of their enemies (Deut 32:22-26). The lake of fire is not mentioned.

These are Old Testament illustrations of what the New Testament believer can expect if he denies Christ. The prospects are **fearful**. It would include losing the reward of being a partner with Christ and reigning with Him in His kingdom.

The believer cannot lose his eternal salvation. But he can suffer severe consequences for his sin. The readers should carefully consider the punishment for denying Christ. If tempted, they should meet with other believers and boldly approach Him to find the grace they need in order to remain faithful to Him.

IV. Closing Words of Encouragement (vv 32-39)

10:32-36. Though the author warns his readers that believers can deny the faith and face God's severe discipline and the loss of rewards, he follows the warning with encouraging words.

He reminds them of their past faithful service to the Lord. They could therefore do so now. In the past, they **joyfully** lost their worldly **goods** in order to obtain **great reward** in the future. They looked for eternal possessions. All of this shows that the author is talking to believers. They needed to maintain **endurance amid** their difficulties.

10:37-39. They should continue to believe that Christ **is coming** again, just as He promised. In fact, it will be in **a little while**. He could return at any moment.

The believer who **draws back** by denying Him will suffer **perdition**. This does not refer to hell, but to the loss of rewards at the Judgment Seat of Christ. When He returns, the readers will stand before the King at that judgment. The life's work of each believer who draws back will be lost and have no eternal value. The faithful believer will experience the salvation of his **soul**. The word for *soul* means his life. His life's work will be greatly rewarded when Christ comes (Mark 8:34-38).

These verses show that a believer can fall away. The one who is righteous, which refers to a believer, can draw back. To avoid that, the author reminded them of what Christ's death had accomplished for them and warned them of the fearful consequences of denying the coming King.

The saving of the believer's life's work is the *salvation* of which the book of Hebrews speaks. The readers were being persecuted by their enemies. But Christ will return and defeat those enemies. The enemies of the readers are the enemies of the coming eternal King. If believers remain faithful to the Lord in this hostile world, He will greatly reward them by allowing them to be His partners for eternity. The works of a faithful life will be saved. The deeds of the unfaithful believer will bring discipline and loss.

WEEK 9

QUESTIONS FOR DISCUSSION

1. **What does 10:1 mean when it says that the Old Testament sacrifices did not make the people *perfect*?**

2. **If the blood of animals did not provide forgiveness (v 4), were the Old Testament believers not forgiven of their sins?**

3. **What does the author mean when he says that believers have been *sanctified once for all* by the offering of Christ (v 10)? Consider all the uses of the word sanctify in the letter (esp. 10:14).**

4. **The author says that Jesus *sat down* after His sacrifice on the cross (v 12) and is *waiting* until His enemies are placed under His feet (v 13). What is the significance of these statements?**

5. **Why can the believer approach Christ in prayer with boldness (vv 19-22)?**

6. What is the *hope* that v 23 says the believer has?

7. What does the author say in vv 24-25 about the importance of meeting with other believers?

8. In v 26, what does the author mean by the phrase *sin willfully*?

9. **What does the author mean when he says that the believer who denies the faith no longer has a sacrifice for sins?**

10. **How can a believer experience a discipline worse than death if he denies the faith (vv 28-29)?**

WEEK 10

The Hall of Faith (Hebrews 11:1-40)

Because of who Christ is and the privileges the believer has, the Christian should live a life of faith. The author gives many examples of people who did. This is not the faith that makes one a Christian. Instead, it is about *living* by faith (10:38). It is a life characterized by obedience, endurance, and, at times, suffering. They lived as they did because they sought to be rewarded for their faithful living in the coming kingdom of God. Any reader of Hebrews can learn a great deal from these men and women of old.

All these people already had eternal life. This chapter explains why they will be rewarded or great in the coming kingdom.

Commentary

I. Introduction (vv 1-3)

11:1-3. Living by faith involves **things hoped for**, which refers to rewards in Christ's kingdom (10:35-37). He has promised to come soon and reward faithfulness. *Faith* means believing in those promises. Others have lived that way and pleased God.

We believe in things we have never seen simply because God says they are so. **By faith** we believe that the **worlds** were created by the **word of God** (v 3). We believe God created the universe and the angelic world. We believe these things even though we were not present to see them happen.

We cannot see the coming kingdom, but we should believe it because God said it will come.

II. God Rewards Faithfulness (vv 4-16)

11:4-6. The author discusses men and women who received God's approval from Creation through the time of Abraham. Righteous **Abel** was murdered. But he **still speaks**. The point is that a life that gains God's approval has an impact that outlasts life on this earth. To those readers facing persecution for their faith, this would be a great source of comfort. They didn't have to fear even death.

Enoch **did not see death**. Whether the child of God dies or the Lord returns to take him in the Rapture, the results of such a life live on. In order to please God, the believer must believe that God is a rewarder of His children who obey Him.

We see the importance of the doctrine of rewards in v 6. It is **impossible** for the believer to **please** God if he doesn't **believe** that God will reward His children if they **seek Him**. If we don't believe in rewards, we call God a liar, because He has said He will reward us for our faithfulness to Him.

11:7-10. Because of his life of faith, Noah received an inheritance. He **became an heir of the righteousness** available to all who come by **faith**. All believers are righteous by faith (10:38). Those believers who draw near to God and believe in things unseen will also become heirs of the rewards God has promised. Noah literally inherited a new world after the Flood. There is a difference between being in the kingdom and inheriting it. Faithful believers will inherit it.

Abraham also looked for an **inheritance**. In this world, he lived in **tents**, not owning the land. But he knew that a **city** with firm **foundations was coming**. This refers to the New Jerusalem, which will be the capital of God's eternal kingdom. It will be an eternal city in an eternal kingdom because the eternal **God** is its **builder** (v 10). Abraham did not worry about owning land in this world. He wanted to own land in an eternal world. The readers should also live in this way.

III. The Faith of the Patriarchs (vv 17-22)

11:17-22. Abraham believed that Isaac would have many descendants because God had said so. Abraham was willing to kill his son when God told him to do so, because he knew that God would **raise him from the dead**. After all, God fulfills His promises.

When **Isaac** was dying, he **blessed** his own sons. These blessings dealt with **things to come**. God had promised the Patriarchs future blessings. Isaac knew that even his death would not prevent these things from coming to fruition. Through his sons, these promises would be realized.

Jacob followed his father's example. **When he was dying**, he had the proper attitude toward God and **worshiped** Him. He did so even though death was imminent. He could do so because he knew God would keep His word. A kingdom was coming in which those who worship the Lord will be rewarded.

Joseph knew that God would reward him in the world to come. He ordered that his **bones** be taken back to the Promised Land because they would be resurrected.

IV. Living by Faith in a Hostile World (vv 23-31)

11:23-29. Moses gave up all the power and riches available to him in Egypt, choosing instead to **suffer affliction**. He gave up the treasures of this world in order to obtain the **reward** Christ will give to those who suffer for Him. Like Abraham, Moses knew that the Christ would come (Deut 18:15).

The Jews ate that first **Passover** meal in Egypt, the land of the enemy. It was a meal that involved the worship of God for all that He was doing for them. The readers were also surrounded by their enemies but were encouraged to continue worshipping Him (10:19-25). God would judge their enemies, just as He judged the Egyptians (1:13; 10:27). They did not need to fear what their enemies could do to them.

The Jewish people were pursued by Pharaoh's army. But God brought them through that time of opposition, delivering them out of Egypt **through the Red Sea**. In faith, the Jews walked through the Sea as God held back the water. God delivers His people who believe He will do so

But those opposed to them died. The Egyptian army **drowned**. They were completely destroyed. This is the destiny of the enemies of the readers of Hebrews as well, even though at that time their enemies appeared to be strong.

11:30-31. The enemies of God were also destroyed at **Jericho**. **Rahab** lived among the enemy, but she was rewarded for her faithfulness to God with the salvation of her life and that of her family.

V. Conclusion (vv 32-39)

11:32-38. The author mentions many more people from the past who remained faithful to the Lord when they faced opposition. In v 32, he even addresses four of the judges. All four of these men had character flaws. They show that God can use any believer and wants to reward all of us.

All these did what they did in order to obtain a **better resurrection** (v 35). All believers will experience resurrection, but faithful believers will experience a better one because they will be partners with Christ in His kingdom.

11:39. All the people in chapter 11 died without receiving the **promise** of being rewarded for their faithfulness. But they did obtain a **good testimony**. In the Greek, ***having obtained a good testimony*** is only one word. It is the same word used in 11:2. It ties together the whole chapter. God was pleased with their lives. They gained God's approval because they trusted Him when He said that those who are faithful to Him will be rewarded with a better resurrection in a world they cannot see (11:1, 35).

The faithful Old Testament believers will not **be made perfect** without the faithful New Testament believers. The Greek word *made perfect* means "to reach a goal." The goal of faithful living is to be greatly rewarded in the kingdom of God. The readers of Hebrews can be rewarded in the same way as the faithful men and women of chapter 11 will be rewarded in the glorious future that is coming.

What a great motivation to live a life of faith! We too can be part of the hall of faith.

WEEK 10

QUESTIONS FOR DISCUSSION

1. How does the author define "faith" in v 1?

2. Why was Abel's sacrifice better than Cain's?

3. **According to v 6, how important is it to understand and believe in the doctrine of rewards?**

4. **Why do you think the author includes Sarah in the hall of faith?**

5. **According to v 16, can God be ashamed of a believer? Why or why not?**

6. What do the lives of the Patriarchs teach about death and rewards in vv 17-22?

____

____

____

____

____

7. According to vv 25-26, what should the readers know about rewards from the life of Moses?

____

____

____

____

____

8. Do you think Rahab is a good addition to the hall of faith (v 31)? Why or why not?

____

____

____

____

____

9. **Why do you think the author discusses the severe suffering that many of these men and women of faith endured (vv 35-38)?**

10. **Comment on the statement in v 38 that the "world was not worthy" of these men and women of faith.**

WEEK 11

A Call to Endure (Hebrews 12:1-29)

The readers should endure and remain faithful to the Lord, just as the men and women of faith in chapter 11 did.

Commentary

I. Introduction (12:1-2)

12:1-2. The people in chapter 11 are **witnesses** and examples for us. If they remained faithful, so can we.

The believer who wants to please the Lord is metaphorically in a **race**. It is difficult. To run it well, we must lay aside anything, including sin, that might weigh us down.

Christ is our ultimate example. For the **joy** of ruling over His kingdom, He suffered on the cross. If we suffer with Him, we will rule with Him.

II. The Importance of Endurance (12:3-11)

12:3-11. If they endure in faithfulness during their times of difficulty, even if it results in **bloodshed**, they will be following in Christ's footsteps. When God allows these difficulties to occur, He is treating believers as **sons**. Therefore, they should **not despise** such things—they should not resent or complain about them. They should not become **discouraged** by them, because they are all a part of the **chastening of the Lord**.

The word *chastening* has the basic meaning of "raising up a child." It refers to all the discipline that a father gives his child in order to teach that child the things he needs to know. It involves all that goes into educating a child. A child becomes a mature son after being trained by his father. That is what God is doing with the readers.

All Christians are children of God. They belong to the family of God. He has given them His life. They have been born from above (John 3:3). Those who suffer with the Lord have matured. These are the believers who will reign with Christ. Not all believers can be called sons of God.

These Christians were in an agonizing race (v 1). They were faced with many opponents. Instead of losing heart, they should be encouraged that all they were going through was the result of God's plan for their benefit. God was training them to be partners with His Son in the coming kingdom.

III. Living Together under the Discipline of God (12:12-17)

12:12-14. The Christian race is not an individual event. We run it with others. We have a responsibility to our fellow believers. We are to meet with other Christians in worship and should meet each other's needs (10:24-25).

Those who are **feeble** and have difficulty running a **straight** line need encouragement. Regularly meeting with other believers allows us to use our gifts for the good of others.

We can also encourage others by obeying the Lord and living a life of **holiness**. We will be like the people in chapter 11. This is the kind of life in which people can **see God** at work in us. If we serve others and remain faithful to the Lord, the world will see Christ in us.

12:15-17. But such a life of holiness is not automatic. There is a danger that we, as well as other Christians around us, will **fall short of the grace of God**.

In Hebrews, and especially here in chapter 12, the author is talking about a Christian who drops out of the race. Through Christ, all believers have God's grace available to enable them to run the race well (4:16). However, a believer can fail to take advantage of that grace. He still has eternal life, but he will not be an encouragement to others and will lose eternal rewards.

Esau is an Old Testament illustration of a believer who falls away. He had the **birthright** of being the firstborn son and gaining a rich inheritance. He gave it away because he did not value it. A bowl of soup was worth more to him when he was hungry.

Esau remained the child of Isaac. But he lost a great reward. Believers can lose the great reward of ruling with Christ, even though they would remain His children and live with Him forever.

Believers need to take seriously the prospect of rewards in the coming kingdom.

IV. The Christian's Great Privileges (12:18-24)

12:18-21. The Christian has great privileges. Throwing those privileges away would have serious consequences. But with the privileges comes great responsibility.

The Old Covenant was given at Mount Sinai. It was a **mountain** that could be **touched**. This speaks of the fact that it belonged to this world. We are reminded that the people of faith in chapter 11 focused on heavenly, not worldly, things.

Under the Old Covenant, the people could not approach God. Such a prospect was terrifying. They **begged** that God **should not** speak **to them**. They asked Moses to speak to God for them (Exod 20:19). But even Moses experienced fear and **trembling** during this encounter.

12:22-24. But it is not that way with the New Testament believer. Unlike the earthly Mount Sinai, the Christian comes to **Mount Zion** (v 22). Mount Zion was the place in Jerusalem where the temple was built. It thus became synonymous with the dwelling place of God.

The author is using *Mount Zion* to represent a heavenly mountain, as opposed to the earthly Mt. Sinai. The earthly mountain could not be touched (v 20). But the Christian can **come to** the greater, heavenly Mount Zion. We can boldly approach His throne. This is unlike the experience of God's people at Sinai. There, they were not able to come to God, instead staying back because of fear (vv 19-21).

The dwelling place of God has innumerable **angels**. When those who will rule with Christ go through difficulties, these angels are sent out to help them (1:14). These angels are part of a **general assembly** (v 23). In Greek, *general assembly* is represented by only one word. It refers to a joyful gathering. The angels are celebrating with the **church of the firstborn**. While many interpret this as a reference to all Christians, the context suggests otherwise.

These words express the joy that faithful believers will experience upon entering the kingdom of God. All believers will be there and have joy. But those who suffered with Christ will hear His approving words: "Well done, good and faithful servant!" There will be a special type of joy for these believers who experience a better resurrection (11:35).

There is a difference between being a child and being a firstborn son. All Christians are children of God, but not all will be rewarded with the rights of a firstborn son. Esau was the firstborn but gave up those rights. *The firstborn* here refers to those who inherit eternal privileges. It refers to those who have run the race well (vv 1-2) and will rule with Christ in His kingdom. The men and women of chapter 11 are examples. When all these partners of Christ arrive in the kingdom, there will be a joyful celebration for them.

V. The Final Warning (12:25-29)

12:25-29. The first warning in Hebrews was found in 2:1-4. In that warning, the author said that the readers needed to give heed to what they had heard. If they did not, they would not escape the consequences. The author now gives his last warning and repeats these themes.

When the people of God received the Old Covenant, they listened with fear and reverence (vv 18-21). New Testament believers have greater privileges than they did. We should listen and respond appropriately.

At Sinai, He spoke to His people from **earth**. In Christ, He speaks to us through the One who is in **heaven** at His right hand (1:13).

The Jews who disobeyed Him under the Old Covenant **did not escape** punishment. How can a New Testament believer expect to **escape** punishment if he does not listen to the King who is seated in the heavens?

God's voice will one day **shake** both **the earth and heaven** (Hag 2:6). Revelation 20:11 and 21:1 speak of the day when God's word will create a new heavens and a new earth.

Everything on this earth is temporary. On the day that God brings in His eternal kingdom, there will be a **removal** of all **things** that are temporary, that is, that can be **shaken** (v 27). God will replace them with things that are permanent and **cannot be shaken**. Ultimately, these are the things that are important.

Verse 28 gives us the purpose of the author's warning. There is only one proper response for the Christian. He should **serve God with reverence and godly fear**. The reason we should do so is that the Christian is in the process of **receiving a kingdom**.

Faithful believers will also *receive the kingdom*. All believers will enter the kingdom. But only faithful believers will actually *receive* it. There is a difference between entering a place and owning a part of it. Faithful believers will receive an inheritance in it. It is an eternal reward that **cannot be shaken**.

WEEK 11

QUESTIONS FOR DISCUSSION

1. **Does Hebrews 12:1 teach that deceased believers are looking down on us?**

2. **What two things does the author say a believer must "lay aside" if he wants to run the Christian "race" well? Why is this sometimes difficult?**

3. **What was the joy set before Jesus on the cross, and what does it mean for believers (v 2)?**

4. **In vv 6-8, what distinguishes those who are sons from those who are illegitimate?**

5. **What are the benefits the author mentions in vv 10-11 for the believer who faithfully endures God's discipline?**

6. What does the author mean when he says that those who do not pursue holiness will not see the Lord (v 14)?

7. Do you think Esau was a believer? Why or why not (vv 16-17)?

8. How would you argue that the "church of the firstborn who are registered in heaven" (v 23) does not refer to all believers, but to those who will be great in the kingdom?

9. **Who do you think are the "just men made perfect" in v 23?**

10. **The author concludes his final warning (vv 25-29) with the reminder that God is a consuming fire. Discuss what this phrase means.**

WEEK 12

Concluding Remarks (Hebrews 13:1-25)

Many New Testament books follow the pattern of discussing doctrine first, then explaining how readers can put that doctrine into practice. Hebrews follows that pattern. The author told the readers to serve God with holy reverence (12:28). Now, he gives them commands that show them how to do that.

Commentary

I. Five Virtues to Cultivate (13:1-6)

13:1-3. The author gives five commandments. The first is that the believer is to love his fellow Christians. That would mean **continu[ing]** to meet with them in worship and encouraging them in the struggles they face (10:24-25).

The second commandment is to **entertain strangers**, which is a way to love other believers. The author probably has in mind traveling first-century Christian teachers. They were dependent on the hospitality of other Christians, who provided lodging and food.

The third commandment is also related to loving other believers. The readers are to **remember the prisoners** (v 3). These readers were experiencing persecution for their faith. Some of their fellow believers were still in prison. The readers had ministered to such people in the past (10:33-34), and should continue to do so.

13:4-6. The fourth commandment deals with sexual immorality. Sexual relations are acceptable to God only in the **marriage bed** (v 4).

The fifth commandment deals with **covetousness**. Christians are to be **content** with what they **have** (v 5). They are not to covet material things.

This was very applicable to the original readers. They had already suffered the loss of material goods because of their faith (10:34). But the author had reminded them that all these things belong to this creation and are only temporary (12:27).

To encourage them in this area, the author quotes from Josh 1:5 and Deut 31:6-7. In those verses, God tells Joshua that as he faces his enemies in the land, God will not **leave nor forsake** him. God will be there in all the difficult times.

II. The Importance of Church Leaders (13:7-17)

13:7-11. The author begins and ends this section by discussing the leaders in the church. In v 7, he refers to the readers' past teachers and, in v 17, the present ones. In between, he reminds the readers that these teachers taught them the doctrines of the Lord. The readers were in danger of forgetting what these men had taught (5:11-14).

These men not only taught well. They lived well. They served God in a pleasing way (12:28). The readers were to **follow** their **faith** and consider **their conduct**. These men, like the examples in chapter 11, lived lives of faith. This shows the importance of godly teachers. Since Jesus is the same **yesterday, today, and forever**, what these sound teachers taught does not change.

Since what their leaders had taught them was still true, they should avoid **various and strange doctrines** (v 9). The new teachings that were luring them away from Christianity were contrary to the truth they had been taught.

Part of the false teaching alluring them away involved **foods**. Judaism placed a great deal of importance on what a person ate. Many teachers within Judaism taught that what we eat can make us closer to God. But growth in our spiritual lives does not occur because of material things such as food. Instead, spiritual growth comes by God's **grace** (Heb 4:16). False teaching, of whatever kind, does not teach the grace of God.

Growth in the Christian life does not occur through keeping a list of legalistic commandments that we check off each day. It comes by being transformed by the Spirit as we take in God's Word and ask Him to change us (2 Cor 3:18; Rom 12:1-2). The readers were being tempted to go back to a system that concentrated on external means of growth.

New Testament believers have a different kind of *food* to eat. Their leaders had taught them about the superiority over Judaism and their privileges in Christ. In Christ, we have a different **altar** from the one of the Old Testament. Old Testament worshippers would often eat from the sacrifices made on the *altar*. The word clearly refers to the death of Christ. In His sacrifice, the Christian is able to find spiritual nourishment. We grow through contact with Him (John 15:4). We go to Him to find the grace and spiritual things we need (v 9; 4:16).

13:12-17. On the Day of Atonement, the priests in the Old Testament did not eat the meat of the animals. The bodies of the **animals** killed on that day were **burned outside the camp** (v 11). The sacrificed animals were taken outside the area where the Jews lived because their dead bodies were considered unclean; they had taken on, in a figurative sense, the sins of the people. By removing the bodies of these animals from their midst, the Jews were saying their sins were an unholy thing. They were symbolically removing everything associated with their sin.

There is a parallel between what happened on the Day of Atonement and the Lord Jesus. Just as those sacrificed animals were taken outside the camp, so **Jesus** died outside the city of Jerusalem and its **gate** (v 12). This is a picture of His being considered unholy and being rejected by the Jews. He was **outside** what Judaism considered good.

But instead of being unholy, Jesus' **blood** had sanctified them. In Heb 10:10, 14, the word **sanctify** was used to describe how Christ's sacrifice had made believers holy forever. This sacrifice results in the gift of eternal life to all who believe in Him for it.

It would be a terrible mistake to return to Judaism. Instead, they should align themselves with Christ. They, too, are to go **outside the camp** (v 13). They should leave Judaism completely behind. They needed to leave all the religious rituals, worship at the temple, and all the things associated with the Old Covenant. The Lord was rejected by the Jews. He died a shameful death. The readers are to stand with Him and share His **reproach**, including any persecution that went with it. A faithful believer will experience the rebuke of the world, no matter where and when he lives.

The readers will appear before the Judgment Seat of Christ. They will give an account of how they submitted to the teaching of their Christian leaders, who taught them the truth. If readers rejected the sound teaching of these leaders and thereby caused them **grief**, they would not benefit from their guidance. In addition, they would suffer loss on the day they appear before Christ.

III. Personal Final Word (13:18-25)

13:18-25. The author prays for the readers. The One he prays to on their behalf is the **God of peace** (v 20). Because of Christ, these readers were at peace with God (Rom 5:1). In the midst of their difficult circumstances, they should be at peace with one another.

The **Lord Jesus** is called the **great Shepherd of the sheep**. In the Old Testament, the king was called the shepherd of his people. Jesus Christ is *the* King of His people.

But as we have seen in Hebrews, Jesus is also His people's High Priest. The **blood** of His sacrifice makes possible all the benefits of the **everlasting Covenant**. It is an eternal covenant, unlike the Old Covenant that it replaced. Under this covenant, God raised Christ **from the dead** after His sacrifice and has seated Him at His right hand, where He serves as our High Priest.

The author prays that God will **make** them **complete in every good work**. This means that God would strengthen them to do **what is pleasing** to Him. God is pleased with the good works of His people (v 16). These works can be done only **through Jesus Christ**. It is in Christ that the believer finds the grace and mercy to serve the Lord and remain faithful to Him (4:14-16).

It is only through the power He provides that one can obtain the reward of reigning with Christ, which is an overarching theme of the book of Hebrews. Such a reward involves sharing in the **glory** of the One who will reign **forever and ever**.

WEEK 12

QUESTIONS FOR DISCUSSION

1. **Did some first-century Christians entertain angels without knowing it (v 2)? Old Testament believers? Do you think this happens in our day?**

2. **What does the author say about sexual purity in v 4?**

3. **In vv 5-6, the author quotes from Josh 1:5 and Deut 31:6-7. Why were these verses relevant to the original readers and any Christian who is faithful to the Lord?**

4. **What would you say to someone who says that because Jesus is always the same, speaking in tongues and the ability to do miracles are for today (v 8)?**

5. **According to vv 15-16, what sacrifices should the Christian offer to God?**

6. **What do you think about the command to obey and be submissive to church leaders (v 17)?**

7. **The book of Hebrews presents Christ as the King of the world to come and the High Priest of believers. How do you think the author refers to these offices of Christ in v 20?**

8. **What does v 21 teach us about good works in the life of the believer?**

9. After studying the book of Hebrews, what do you think about eternal rewards in the coming kingdom of Christ?

10. What would you say to those who say that Hebrews teaches that believers can lose their salvation? How does your answer depend on what the author of Hebrews meant by *salvation*?

Made in the USA
Coppell, TX
22 June 2026

82818762R00059